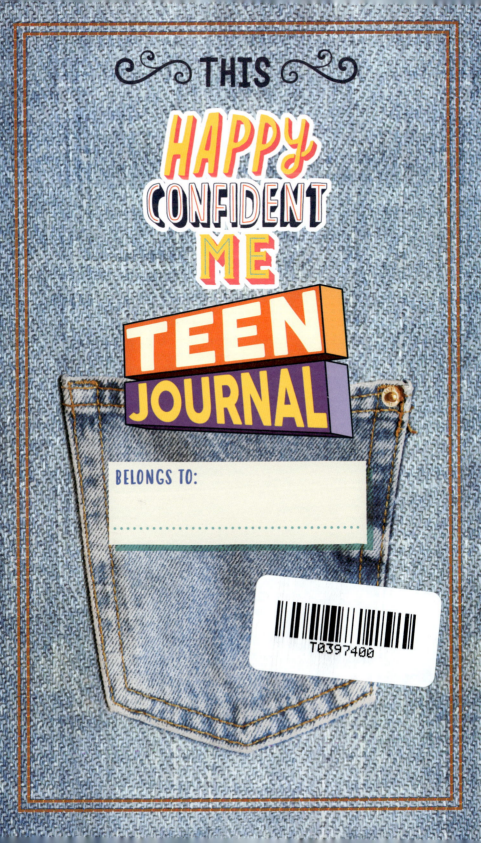

First published in Great Britain by The Happy Confident Company,
January 2025

Copyright © The Happy Confident Company Ltd. 2025
www.happyconfident.com

Authors: Nadim Saad & Jo Chadwick

The authors assert their moral right to be identified as the authors of this work.

All rights reserved. No part of this publication may be reproduced, stored in a retrieval system, transmitted in any form or by any means, electronic, mechanical, photocopying, recording or otherwise, without the prior permission of the publishers.

ISBN: 9781068543807

Design and Illustration by Daniel Bobroff, Electric Design Studio Ltd

Printed and bound in China.

The Happy Confident Me: Teen Journal is written and published as a resource and guide to help teenagers create positive daily habits to equip them with skills to help them flourish and thrive. Although every effort has been made to ensure the contents of this book are accurate, the information provided is not meant to take the place of professional psychiatric advice from professionals. Please consult your doctor, social worker or the safeguarding officer at your child's school if you are concerned about your child's mental health or emotional wellbeing. The authors cannot be held responsible for any loss or damage suffered as a result of complete reliance on any part of this book's contents or any errors or omissions herein.

DEDICATION

This journal is dedicated to all teens everywhere to help you build the tools and strategies to become the best versions of yourself.

Remember to always be kind to yourself and know that the biggest changes can be made by taking a series of small, manageable steps. Don't forget to take time to reflect on the good, and celebrate your success, and look upon your challenges and mistakes as opportunities to grow.

But over and above everything else, take life a day at a time, looking for the goodness in even the smallest of things. Your teenage years will be filled with mixed emotions, highs and lows, but they're all part of the journey to becoming the person you want to be.

Wishing you a future-filled with happiness, confidence and positive vibes.

Nadim Jo xx

WHAT'S INSIDE

INSIDE FRONT **GLOSSARY OF FEELINGS**
With 40 feelings and definitions, this is a great reference point to help you capture your feelings of the day.

P.6 CREATING POSITIVE DAILY HABITS
Find out why creating positive daily habits will set you up for success in life and discover the simple tools to achieve this success. Plus... learn how your brain creates habits, and how to exercise your neural pathways to deliver positive outcomes.

P.8 CONQUERING NEGATIVE THOUGHTS
Get to grips with the fact that the human brain is wired for negative thinking and learn how to turn off your inner doubts, transforming your self-belief.

P.10 BECOMING THE PERSON YOU WANT TO BE
It's time to self-reflect on where you're at right now in life. What's going well and what's holding you back? This activity will help you consider the person you choose to be, so you'll be able to focus on that vision when setting your habits.

P.12 HOW TO USE YOUR JOURNAL
Discover how you can make the most of your journaling experience with this handy guide explaining each of the areas that you'll consider each day. Learn how to better define your feelings by using the FEELIT® Mapper and understand the role that practising daily gratitude plays in helping you become happier and more confident.

4

P.15 JOURNALING PAGES

70 days of daily structured journaling to help you become the best version of yourself. With interesting quotes and motivating affirmations each day, there is always something extra to help build your happiness and confidence.

Something you want to delve into detail about? There's a whole page each day where you can expand on any areas of your day.

EVERY 10 DAYS
REFLECT & RESET

Every 10 journaling days you will find an activity to help you to reflect on the past 10 days, look at what's gone well, and what challenges you may have faced (and even overcome) and celebrate your successes. You can take stock of your feelings, and assess your positive daily habits and focus moving forward.

P.170 FINAL REFLECTION

At the end of your journal you'll find a handy section to reflect on your entire journaling experience capturing what you've discovered about your feelings, your challenges and successes. This simple activity will help you determine what steps you want to take next on your journey to becoming the best version of yourself.

INSIDE BACK — HABIT TRACKER

Tucked away into the back of your journal you'll find your 70 day habit tracker.

Broken into 7 blocks of 10 days you can track up to 5 habits each week. Either carry them through to the next week, or set yourself some new goals. It's totally flexible.

CREATING POSITIVE DAILY HABITS

What do you think about when you hear the word HABIT?

Perhaps you think of biting your nails, having a messy bedroom, interrupting people, or perhaps certain words that you can't help repeating on a daily basis. You'd be right, any regular patterns that you would find hard to give up, are indeed a habit.

But one thing we often don't consider is that it's not just our actions that are habits, but also our thoughts, and feelings.

The older we get, the more habits we pick up, so when you hit your teens and enter into puberty, you're starting to form the basis of your character. And at this point, the more self-aware and self-accepting you are, the more you can focus your energy on becoming the adult you want to become one day.

Take a moment to make a list of the things you like about yourself, your best friend, and an adult you really respect.

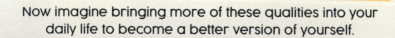

Now imagine bringing more of these qualities into your daily life to become a better version of yourself.

Now, let's look at how the brain develops and at **NEURAL PATHWAYS**. Our brains are continually building new neural pathways, building new habits, and working to make the things we focus our attention on doing, easier.

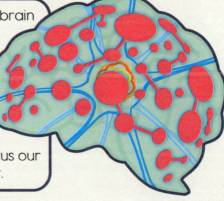

Think of it this way... the route you walk or drive to school each day is probably the same. You almost don't even notice the journey because it's so familiar. Let's say the regular road was cut off tomorrow...and you needed to find a new route. Sure, it'd be strange for a couple of days, feel like it's taking ages to get there, but the more time you travel that route, the more familiar it'll become, until, like the first route, you don't even notice the journey.

So habits are made by pushing our brains to try new things, and keep on doing them until it's second nature.

Now reflecting on the journey from teen to young adult, you are totally in control of the person you are, and the one you want to become. It's all about creating the right, positive daily habits.

> "Watch your thoughts, they become your words; watch your words, they become your actions; watch your actions, they become your habits; watch your habits, they become your character; watch your character, it becomes your destiny."
>
> Lao Tzu

CONQUERING NEGATIVE THOUGHTS

Did you know the human brain is actually wired to focus on negative thoughts?

This is our "default mode" and the brain has evolved this way to help look for signs of danger and protect us.

However, our 'default network' can be really quite noisy and disruptive at times throwing all kinds of thoughts at us, some helpful, and some unhelpful.

Think about daydreaming...you know, when you get lost in the moment and let your imagination run wild. These are thoughts we enjoy, they might even entertain us – We don't treat them as truths...do we?

So why is it, that when we have negative thoughts, or inner doubts, we almost always treat these with concern and let them affect us? Strange isn't it!

So, in the same way as we don't believe in every daydream, we also don't need to believe our inner doubts either...and certainly not allow them to pull us down. They're just thoughts after all, not necessarily truths.

In fact, you can train your brain to focus on the good stuff instead of getting stuck on the bad.

Here are three scientifically proven ways...

⬡ GRATITUDE

Gratitude helps you see the positives in your life and shifts your focus away from the negatives. Conquer the art of gratitude simply by writing down three things a day that you're thankful for.

⬡ CELEBRATE SMALL WINS

Did you complete your homework? Help a friend? Every tiny success matters so celebrate them! You'll soon notice that your achievements boost your confidence and you'll have that great feeling of moving forwards, even in small steps.

⬡ REFRAME NEGATIVE THOUGHTS

Switch on your inner detective and listen out for those negative thoughts and when you spot them, flip them into something more helpful. For example, if you think, "I'll never get this right," reframe it to, "I'm still learning, and I'll get there."

By simply applying these three steps on an ongoing basis, you'll train your brain to become more positive.

And guess what...people who think more positively are proven to be happier, healthier, and more successful.

And this journal is going to help you do just that!

BECOMING THE PERSON I WANT TO BE

To give yourself the very best chance of becoming the person you wish to be when you're older, you need to start with understanding who you are today and think about the habits you have that are not helpful to you.

Now this isn't about wanting material things, money, tech, or games, it's about the person you are, how you feel about yourself and how you want others to feel about you.

Consider fears that might hold you back, ways you act sometimes that you often regret, negative views of yourself that you know aren't helping you, and challenges you wish you didn't struggle with.

Understand the effect your thoughts and feelings have on your actions – forming new positive daily habits is key to becoming the very best version of yourself. Starting this journey means identifying the habits that you want to focus on over the next few months, letting go of the ones that don't serve you and replacing them with more useful habits that will serve you better.

On the next page, you'll see two columns, one titled **WHERE I'M AT**, and the other **WHERE I WANT TO BE**.

Follow the stages below to complete this exercise...

1. Start on the left **WHERE I'M AT** column and try to think of up to three habits you have that hold you back the most. Think of the ones that regularly cause you problems. It could be tough to write these down because it's natural to struggle to accept parts of us we want to change. But once you are able to identify them, and own them, you can then be empowered to change them.

2. Next move to the **WHERE I WANT TO BE** column. Against each **WHERE I'M AT** statement, write down how you'd like to change. This may just be one word, like **PATIENT**, **FOCUSED**, or **CONFIDENT** or it might be a longer sentence. Spend some time on this though...the more you consider it at the start, the more focused you can be on achieving it!

WHERE I'M AT	WHERE I WANT TO BE

When you're done, look at your **WHERE I WANT TO BE** statements. Close your eyes and imagine yourself as you become more and more like these statements. Imagine how you'd feel when you wake up in the mornings, imagine how you'd act with your family, and friends. And know that you can get there, not overnight, but with focus on this development goal. This journal is going to help you transform your habits taking you closer to the version of yourself that you want to become.

Now go to your Habit Tracker on page 176 and write down some of the positive habits that will help you become your best self.

LET THE JOURNEY BEGIN!

HOW TO USE YOUR JOURNAL

> This journal provides you with 70 days of structured journaling, designed to help you focus some time each day around your own personal development.

By using tthis journal for less than 10 minutes a day...you will:
Understand yourself better • Become more focused on achieving your dreams • Better understand your emotions • Understand the effect your feelings have on your thoughts and actions and • Form new positive daily habits.

A DAILY CHANCE TO REFLECT ON YOUR FEELINGS

All feelings can be grouped into one of 4 quadrants...each representing feeling types and helping us distinguish our feelings based on both energy levels, and whether these sensations FEEL pleasant or unpleasant in our bodies. Our FEELIT® Mapper will help you better understand how you're feeling...

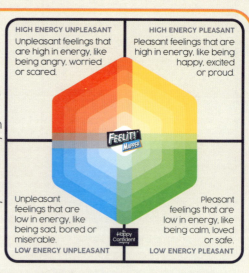

HIGH ENERGY UNPLEASANT
Unpleasant feelings that are high in energy, like being angry, worried or scared.

HIGH ENERGY PLEASANT
Pleasant feelings that are high in energy, like being happy, excited or proud.

LOW ENERGY UNPLEASANT
Unpleasant feelings that are low in energy, like being sad, bored or miserable.

LOW ENERGY PLEASANT
Pleasant feelings that are low in energy, like being calm, loved or safe.

Each day reflect on all of your feelings and mark them on to the daily mini mapper. Note that the colours are lighter in the centre, and darker on the outside rings. The darker the colour, the MORE you're feeling that feeling. Use the free space provided to list your feelings or write about them in more detail, think about what happened during the day that activated these feelings.

For inspiration and to help you dig deeper into your feelings, use the glossary on the inside front cover of this journal.

THINGS I FOUND DIFFICULT
Reflecting on the day, what has been tough or challenged you the most?

THINGS THAT WENT WELL
This section gives you an opportunity to celebrate yourself each day. Make a record of something you've done that's gone well, a goal you've set that you've achieved, helping a friend in need, or cracking something that's been a real challenge.

THREE THINGS I'M GRATEFUL FOR
Finding and listing three good things a day is a scientifically proven technique that will increase your happiness levels and also optimism. It's the basis of the practice of gratitude. Your three things can be simple. It's all about noticing the small things every day that make our lives better. The sun shining, a long bath, a call from a friend, a nice meal or someone who's been kind to you.

HABIT TRACKING
Head to the back cover of your journal and tick off the habits that you've achieved each day. See P.176 to define your habits.

REFLECTIONS OF THE DAY
This page provides you with the space to write about anything, capturing things that you might want to think through or remember in future.

Consider the effect your thoughts and feelings had on your day and any techniques you may have used to help yourself stay on track with your goals and habits.

REFLECT & RESET

Every 10 days there is a page that asks you to consider the past 10 days, what's been going well, what you want to do more of, what you want to do less of.

Consider the following:

YOUR FEELINGS
Look back at your feelings: do you see any patterns? Eg. if you have a lot of Blue or Red feelings, what can you do to create more Green and Yellow feelings?

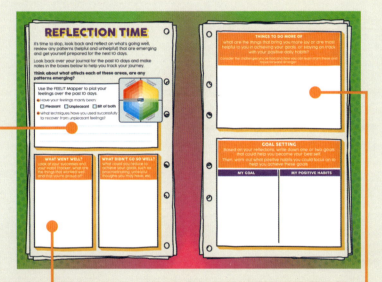

ACHIEVEMENTS
Take some time to celebrate all of your achievements. How can you ensure that you keep having achievements to celebrate?

YOUR HABIT TRACKING
How's it going? Has it been easy? Or if it's been tricky to stick to habits. Are you perhaps trying to do too much, or trying to instil change too quickly? How can you help yourself reset trickier habits by breaking them into more achievable ones? Do you want to carry over tracking the same habits for another 10 days and/or would you like to add some new ones into the mix?

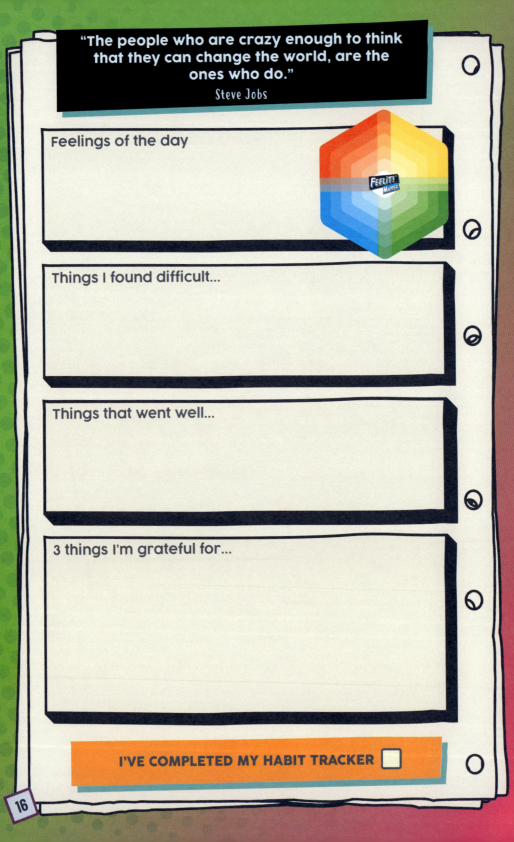

REFLECTIONS OF THE DAY

Today is a new day. I will take the positives from yesterday forwards, and leave behind those which do not serve me well.

Feelings of the day

Things I found difficult...

Things that went well...

3 things I'm grateful for...

I'VE COMPLETED MY HABIT TRACKER ☐

REFLECTIONS OF THE DAY

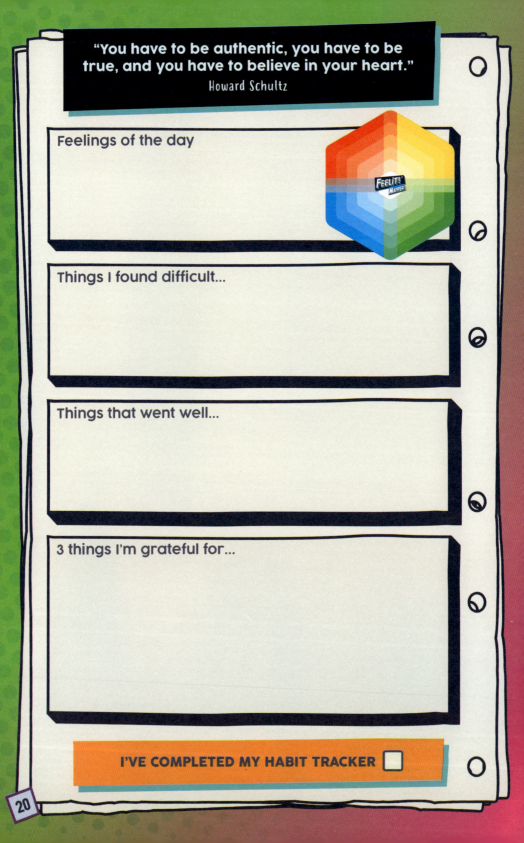

REFLECTIONS OF THE DAY

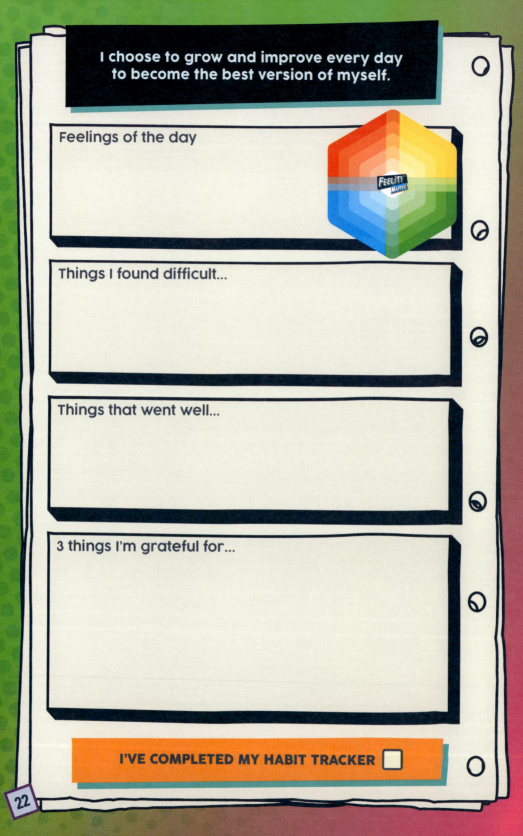

REFLECTIONS OF THE DAY

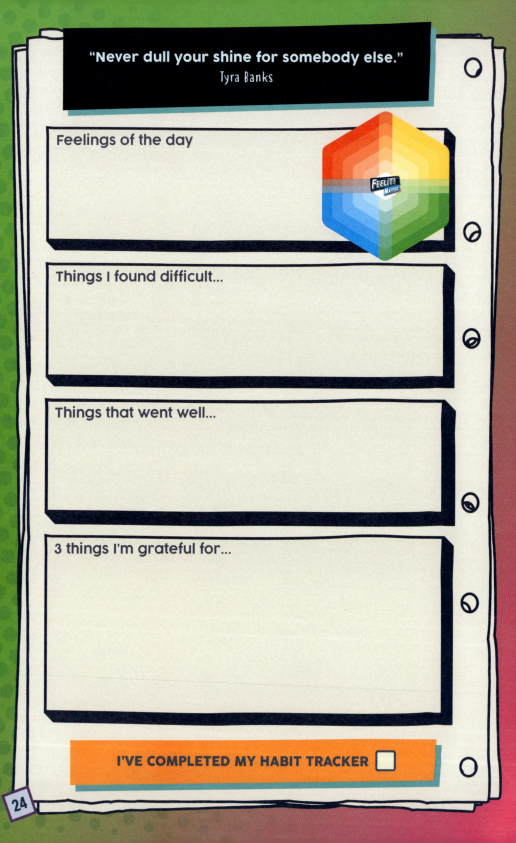

REFLECTIONS OF THE DAY

Today I will value myself, my time and my energy and be grateful for everything I am able to achieve.

Feelings of the day

Things I found difficult...

Things that went well...

3 things I'm grateful for...

I'VE COMPLETED MY HABIT TRACKER ☐

REFLECTIONS OF THE DAY

> "Love yourself. Forgive yourself. Be true to yourself. Because how you treat yourself sets the standard for how others treat you."
> Steve Maraboli

Feelings of the day

Things I found difficult...

Things that went well...

3 things I'm grateful for...

I'VE COMPLETED MY HABIT TRACKER ☐

REFLECTIONS OF THE DAY

I have the power to push myself out of my comfort zone and achieve great things.

Feelings of the day

Things I found difficult...

Things that went well...

3 things I'm grateful for...

I'VE COMPLETED MY HABIT TRACKER ☐

REFLECTIONS OF THE DAY

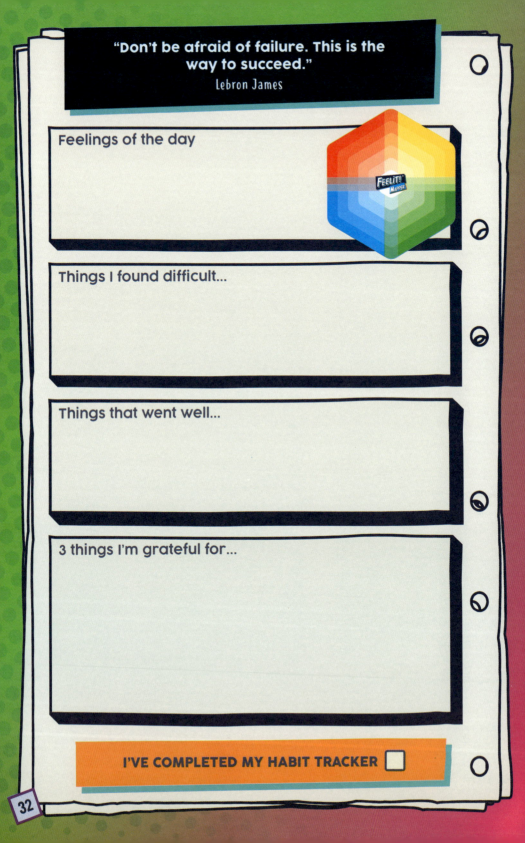

REFLECTIONS OF THE DAY

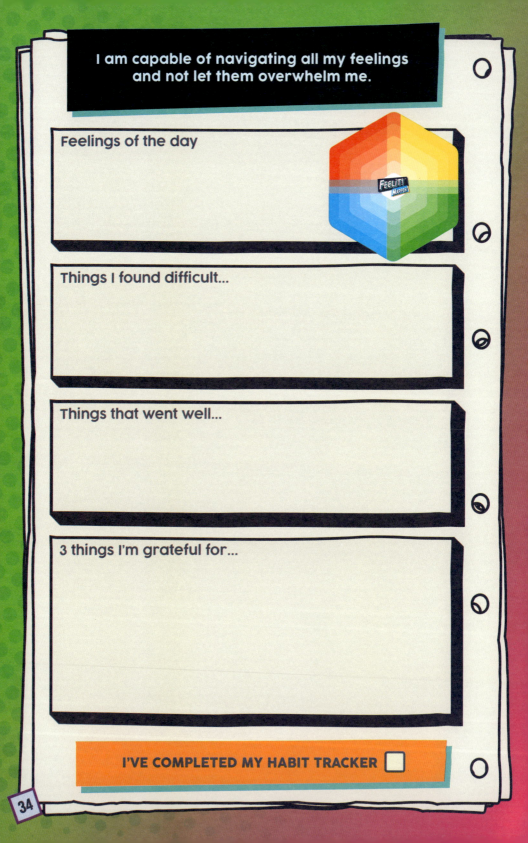

REFLECTIONS OF THE DAY

REFLECTION TIME

It's time to stop, look back and reflect on what's going well, review any patterns (helpful and unhelpful) that are emerging and get yourself prepared for the next 10 days.

Look back over your journal for the past 10 days and make notes in the boxes below to help you track your journey.

Think about what affects each of these areas, are any patterns emerging?

Use the FEELIT Mapper to plot your feelings over the past 10 days.

- Have your feelings mainly been:
  ☐ Pleasant ☐ Unpleasant ☐ Bit of both
- What techniques have you used successfully to recover from unpleasant feelings?

....
....
....

WHAT WENT WELL?
Look at your successes and your Habit Tracker, what are the things that worked well and that you're proud of?

WHAT DIDN'T GO SO WELL?
What could you reduce to achieve your goals, such as procrastinating, unhelpful thoughts you may have, etc...

THINGS TO DO MORE OF

What are the things that bring you more joy or are most helpful to you in achieving your goals, or staying on track with your positive daily habits?

Consider the challenges you've had and how you can learn from these and move forward stronger.

GOAL SETTING

Based on your reflections, write down one or two goals that could help you become your best self.

Then, work out what positive habits you could focus on to help you achieve these goals.

MY GOAL	MY POSITIVE HABITS

Today will be a great day. I shall see the goodness in all that I do.

Feelings of the day

Things I found difficult...

Things that went well...

3 things I'm grateful for...

I'VE COMPLETED MY HABIT TRACKER ☐

REFLECTIONS OF THE DAY

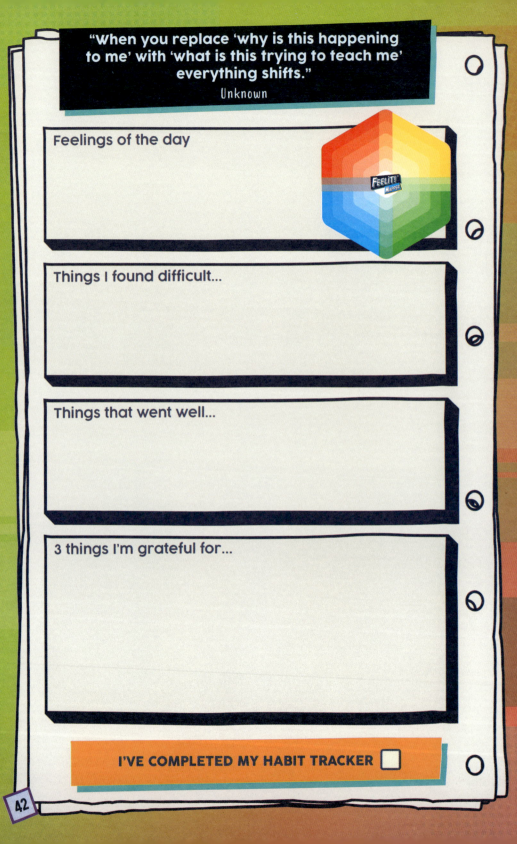

> "When you replace 'why is this happening to me' with 'what is this trying to teach me' everything shifts."
> Unknown

Feelings of the day

Things I found difficult...

Things that went well...

3 things I'm grateful for...

I'VE COMPLETED MY HABIT TRACKER ☐

42

REFLECTIONS OF THE DAY

It's a beautiful day and I welcome it with joy and confidence.

Feelings of the day

Things I found difficult...

Things that went well...

3 things I'm grateful for...

I'VE COMPLETED MY HABIT TRACKER ☐

REFLECTIONS OF THE DAY

> "Resilience is knowing that you are the only one that has the power and the responsibility to pick yourself up."
> Mary Holloway

Feelings of the day

Things I found difficult...

Things that went well...

3 things I'm grateful for...

I'VE COMPLETED MY HABIT TRACKER ☐

REFLECTIONS OF THE DAY

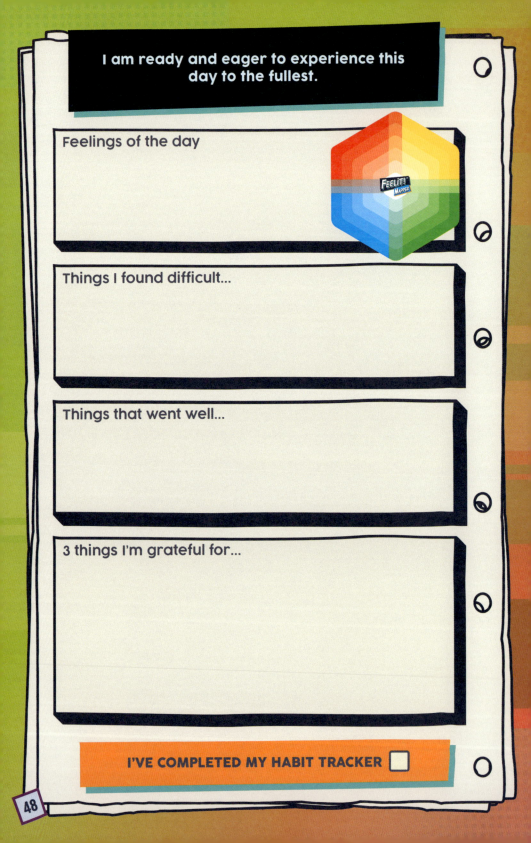

REFLECTIONS OF THE DAY

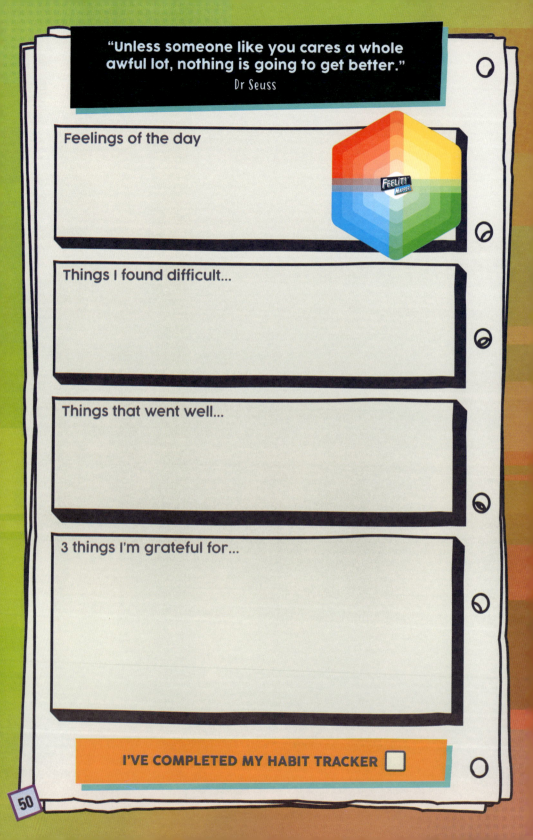

I have the strength to accept my anger and to express it without being hurtful.

Feelings of the day

Things I found difficult...

Things that went well...

3 things I'm grateful for...

I'VE COMPLETED MY HABIT TRACKER ☐

> "Young people willing to push super hard to make something happen are among the most powerful forces in the world."
>
> San Altman

Feelings of the day

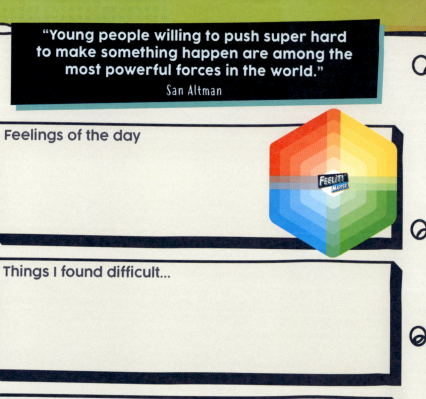

Things I found difficult...

Things that went well...

3 things I'm grateful for...

I'VE COMPLETED MY HABIT TRACKER ☐

REFLECTIONS OF THE DAY

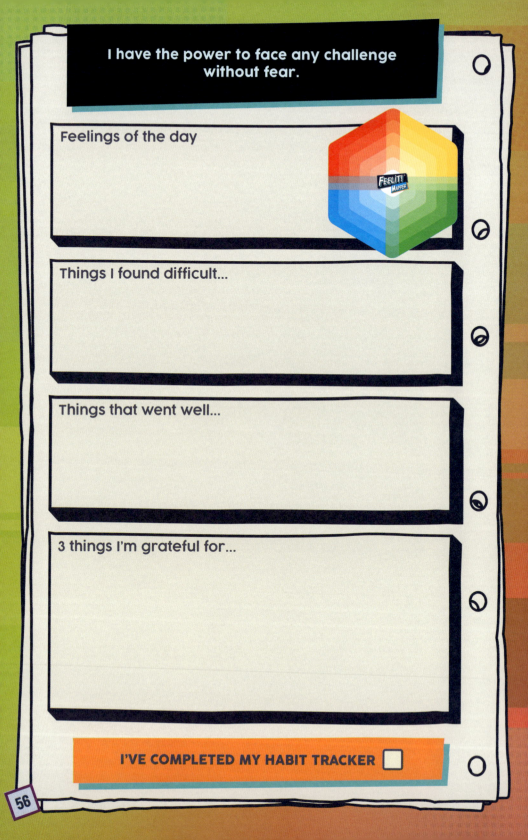

REFLECTIONS OF THE DAY

REFLECTION TIME

It's time to stop, look back and reflect on what's going well, review any patterns (helpful and unhelpful) that are emerging and get yourself prepared for the next 10 days.

Look back over your journal for the past 10 days and make notes in the boxes below to help you track your journey.

Think about what affects each of these areas, are any patterns emerging?

Use the FEELIT Mapper to plot your feelings over the past 10 days.

➡ Have your feelings mainly been:

☐ **Pleasant** ☐ **Unpleasant** ☐ **Bit of both**

➡ What techniques have you used successfully to recover from unpleasant feelings?

....

....

....

WHAT WENT WELL?
Look at your successes and your Habit Tracker, what are the things that worked well and that you're proud of?

WHAT DIDN'T GO SO WELL?
What could you reduce to achieve your goals, such as procrastinating, unhelpful thoughts you may have, etc...

THINGS TO DO MORE OF

What are the things that bring you more joy or are most helpful to you in achieving your goals, or staying on track with your positive daily habits?

Consider the challenges you've had and how you can learn from these and move forward stronger.

GOAL SETTING

Based on your reflections, write down one or two goals that could help you become your best self.

Then, work out what positive habits you could focus on to help you achieve these goals.

MY GOAL	MY POSITIVE HABITS

> "We should all celebrate our individuality and not be embarrassed or ashamed of it."
> Jonny Depp

Feelings of the day

Things I found difficult...

Things that went well...

3 things I'm grateful for...

I'VE COMPLETED MY HABIT TRACKER ☐

60

REFLECTIONS OF THE DAY

I feel positive about myself and everything I will do today.

Feelings of the day

Things I found difficult...

Things that went well...

3 things I'm grateful for...

I'VE COMPLETED MY HABIT TRACKER ☐

> "May your choices reflect your hopes, not your fears."
> Nelson Mandela

Feelings of the day

Things I found difficult...

Things that went well...

3 things I'm grateful for...

I'VE COMPLETED MY HABIT TRACKER ☐

64

REFLECTIONS OF THE DAY

Today I will be open, freely expressing my feelings and emotions.

Feelings of the day

Things I found difficult...

Things that went well...

3 things I'm grateful for...

I'VE COMPLETED MY HABIT TRACKER ☐

REFLECTIONS OF THE DAY

> "When everything seems to be going against you, remember...the airplane takes off against the wind, not with it."
> Henry Ford

Feelings of the day

Things I found difficult...

Things that went well...

3 things I'm grateful for...

I'VE COMPLETED MY HABIT TRACKER ☐

REFLECTIONS OF THE DAY

I will accept everything that happens to me today and will try to see the positive in every situation.

Feelings of the day

Things I found difficult...

Things that went well...

3 things I'm grateful for...

I'VE COMPLETED MY HABIT TRACKER ☐

> "Hard days are the best because that's when champions are made. If you push through the hard days, then you can get through anything."
> Gabby Douglas

Feelings of the day

Things I found difficult...

Things that went well...

3 things I'm grateful for...

I'VE COMPLETED MY HABIT TRACKER ☐

REFLECTIONS OF THE DAY

Today I shield myself from other people's negative comments and thoughts.

Feelings of the day

Things I found difficult...

Things that went well...

3 things I'm grateful for...

I'VE COMPLETED MY HABIT TRACKER ☐

REFLECTIONS OF THE DAY

> "There are always going to be bad things. But you can write it down and make a song out of it."
> Billie Eilish

Feelings of the day

Things I found difficult...

Things that went well...

3 things I'm grateful for...

I'VE COMPLETED MY HABIT TRACKER ☐

REFLECTIONS OF THE DAY

I choose to celebrate my achievements no matter how small.

Feelings of the day

Things I found difficult...

Things that went well...

3 things I'm grateful for...

I'VE COMPLETED MY HABIT TRACKER ☐

REFLECTIONS OF THE DAY

REFLECTION TIME

It's time to stop, look back and reflect on what's going well, review any patterns (helpful and unhelpful) that are emerging and get yourself prepared for the next 10 days.

Look back over your journal for the past 10 days and make notes in the boxes below to help you track your journey.

Think about what affects each of these areas, are any patterns emerging?

Use the FEELIT Mapper to plot your feelings over the past 10 days.

➡ Have your feelings mainly been:

☐ **Pleasant**   ☐ **Unpleasant**   ☐ **Bit of both**

➡ What techniques have you used successfully to recover from unpleasant feelings?

WHAT WENT WELL?
Look at your successes and your Habit Tracker, what are the things that worked well and that you're proud of?

WHAT DIDN'T GO SO WELL?
What could you reduce to achieve your goals, such as procrastinating, unhelpful thoughts you may have, etc...

THINGS TO DO MORE OF

What are the things that bring you more joy or are most helpful to you in achieving your goals, or staying on track with your positive daily habits?

Consider the challenges you've had and how you can learn from these and move forward stronger.

GOAL SETTING

Based on your reflections, write down one or two goals that could help you become your best self.

Then, work out what positive habits you could focus on to help you achieve these goals.

MY GOAL	MY POSITIVE HABITS

> "We must always set the bar high otherwise we don't progress."
> Kylian Mbappe

Feelings of the day

Things I found difficult...

Things that went well...

3 things I'm grateful for...

I'VE COMPLETED MY HABIT TRACKER ☐

REFLECTIONS OF THE DAY

I will do my best not to criticise myself and others today.

Feelings of the day

Things I found difficult...

Things that went well...

3 things I'm grateful for...

I'VE COMPLETED MY HABIT TRACKER ☐

REFLECTIONS OF THE DAY

> "There's a lot of us out here that are birds, man. We all just need to learn to fly."
> Travis Scott

Feelings of the day

Things I found difficult...

Things that went well...

3 things I'm grateful for...

I'VE COMPLETED MY HABIT TRACKER ☐

REFLECTIONS OF THE DAY

I choose to accept my mistakes today and to learn from them.

Feelings of the day

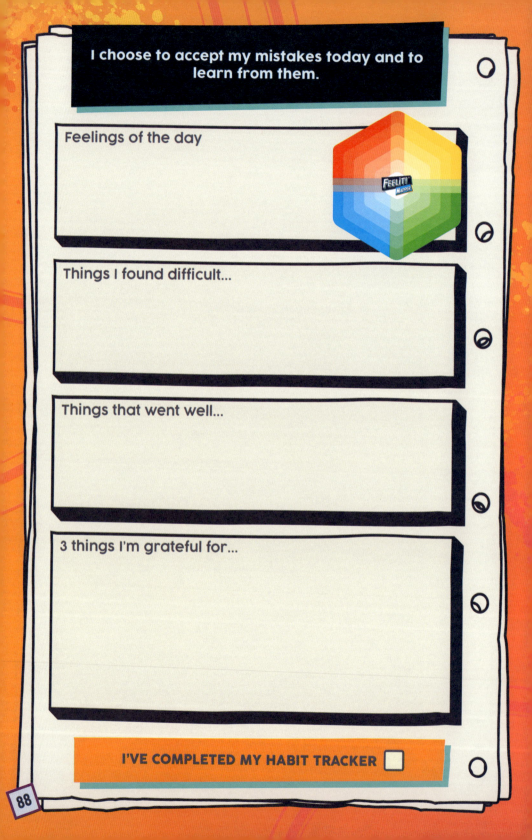

Things I found difficult...

Things that went well...

3 things I'm grateful for...

I'VE COMPLETED MY HABIT TRACKER ☐

REFLECTIONS OF THE DAY

REFLECTIONS OF THE DAY

I realise that everything I need is already around me.

Feelings of the day

Things I found difficult...

Things that went well...

3 things I'm grateful for...

I'VE COMPLETED MY HABIT TRACKER ☐

REFLECTIONS OF THE DAY

> "I raise up my voice – not so I can shout but so that those without a voice can be heard... we cannot succeed when half of us are held back."
>
> Malala Yousafzai

Feelings of the day

Things I found difficult...

Things that went well...

3 things I'm grateful for...

I'VE COMPLETED MY HABIT TRACKER ☐

REFLECTIONS OF THE DAY

I feel safe, protected and cared for.

Feelings of the day

Things I found difficult...

Things that went well...

3 things I'm grateful for...

I'VE COMPLETED MY HABIT TRACKER ☐

REFLECTIONS OF THE DAY

REFLECTIONS OF THE DAY

I choose to feel good about myself and accepted for who I am.

Feelings of the day

Things I found difficult...

Things that went well...

3 things I'm grateful for...

I'VE COMPLETED MY HABIT TRACKER ☐

REFLECTIONS OF THE DAY

REFLECTION TIME

It's time to stop, look back and reflect on what's going well, review any patterns (helpful and unhelpful) that are emerging and get yourself prepared for the next 10 days.

Look back over your journal for the past 10 days and make notes in the boxes below to help you track your journey.

Think about what affects each of these areas, are any patterns emerging?

Use the FEELIT Mapper to plot your feelings over the past 10 days.

➡ Have your feelings mainly been:

☐ **Pleasant**   ☐ **Unpleasant**   ☐ **Bit of both**

➡ What techniques have you used successfully to recover from unpleasant feelings?

WHAT WENT WELL?

Look at your successes and your Habit Tracker, what are the things that worked well and that you're proud of?

WHAT DIDN'T GO SO WELL?

What could you reduce to achieve your goals, such as procrastinating, unhelpful thoughts you may have, etc...

THINGS TO DO MORE OF

What are the things that bring you more joy or are most helpful to you in achieving your goals, or staying on track with your positive daily habits?

Consider the challenges you've had and how you can learn from these and move forward stronger.

GOAL SETTING

Based on your reflections, write down one or two goals that could help you become your best self.

Then, work out what positive habits you could focus on to help you achieve these goals.

MY GOAL	MY POSITIVE HABITS

> "The world is full of magic things, patiently waiting for our senses to grow sharper."
> WB Yeats

Feelings of the day

Things I found difficult...

Things that went well...

3 things I'm grateful for...

I'VE COMPLETED MY HABIT TRACKER ☐

REFLECTIONS OF THE DAY

I will show patience and accept that some things take time.

Feelings of the day

Things I found difficult...

Things that went well...

3 things I'm grateful for...

I'VE COMPLETED MY HABIT TRACKER ☐

> **"Creativity takes courage."**
> Henri Matisse

Feelings of the day

Things I found difficult...

Things that went well...

3 things I'm grateful for...

I'VE COMPLETED MY HABIT TRACKER ☐

REFLECTIONS OF THE DAY

I choose to accept all my feelings and different parts of myself.

Feelings of the day

Things I found difficult...

Things that went well...

3 things I'm grateful for...

I'VE COMPLETED MY HABIT TRACKER ☐

REFLECTIONS OF THE DAY

> "Be yourself; everyone else is already taken."
> Oscar Wilde

Feelings of the day

Things I found difficult...

Things that went well...

3 things I'm grateful for...

I'VE COMPLETED MY HABIT TRACKER ☐

REFLECTIONS OF THE DAY

I choose to be thankful for all the good things I will experience today.

Feelings of the day

Things I found difficult...

Things that went well...

3 things I'm grateful for...

I'VE COMPLETED MY HABIT TRACKER ☐

REFLECTIONS OF THE DAY

> "The mind is everything. What you think, you become."
> Buddha

Feelings of the day

Things I found difficult...

Things that went well...

3 things I'm grateful for...

I'VE COMPLETED MY HABIT TRACKER ☐

REFLECTIONS OF THE DAY

I choose to be open minded and curious about people and things around me.

Feelings of the day

Things I found difficult...

Things that went well...

3 things I'm grateful for...

I'VE COMPLETED MY HABIT TRACKER ☐

REFLECTIONS OF THE DAY

> "All our dreams can come true – if we have the courage to pursue them."
> Walt Disney

Feelings of the day

Things I found difficult...

Things that went well...

3 things I'm grateful for...

I'VE COMPLETED MY HABIT TRACKER ☐

REFLECTIONS OF THE DAY

I will focus on positive things today, and will not let negative things affect me.

Feelings of the day

Things I found difficult...

Things that went well...

3 things I'm grateful for...

I'VE COMPLETED MY HABIT TRACKER ☐

REFLECTIONS OF THE DAY

REFLECTION TIME

It's time to stop, look back and reflect on what's going well, review any patterns (helpful and unhelpful) that are emerging and get yourself prepared for the next 10 days.

Look back over your journal for the past 10 days and make notes in the boxes below to help you track your journey.

Think about what affects each of these areas, are any patterns emerging?

Use the FEELIT Mapper to plot your feelings over the past 10 days.

➡ Have your feelings mainly been:

☐ **Pleasant**   ☐ **Unpleasant**   ☐ **Bit of both**

➡ What techniques have you used successfully to recover from unpleasant feelings?

HIGH ENERGY UNPLEASANT | HIGH ENERGY PLEASANT
LOW ENERGY UNPLEASANT | LOW ENERGY PLEASANT

FEELIT

WHAT WENT WELL?
Look at your successes and your Habit Tracker, what are the things that worked well and that you're proud of?

WHAT DIDN'T GO SO WELL?
What could you reduce to achieve your goals, such as procrastinating, unhelpful thoughts you may have, etc...

THINGS TO DO MORE OF

What are the things that bring you more joy or are most helpful to you in achieving your goals, or staying on track with your positive daily habits?

Consider the challenges you've had and how you can learn from these and move forward stronger.

GOAL SETTING

Based on your reflections, write down one or two goals that could help you become your best self.

Then, work out what positive habits you could focus on to help you achieve these goals.

MY GOAL	MY POSITIVE HABITS

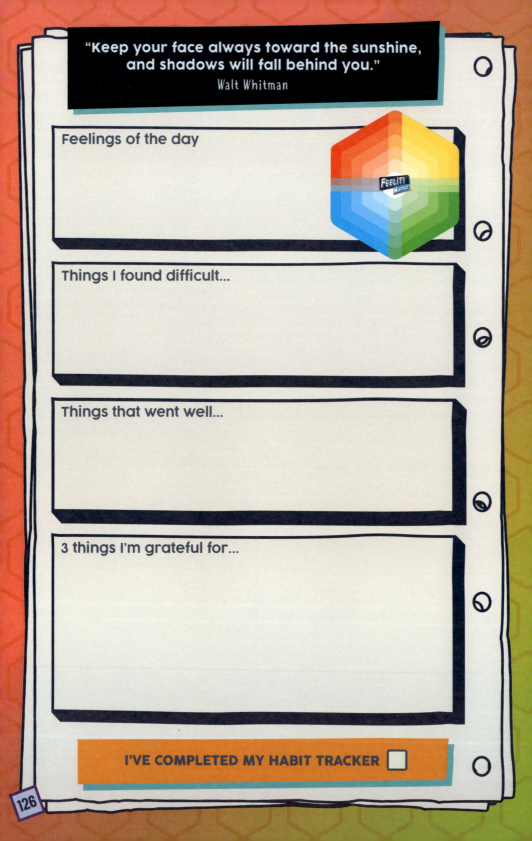

REFLECTIONS OF THE DAY

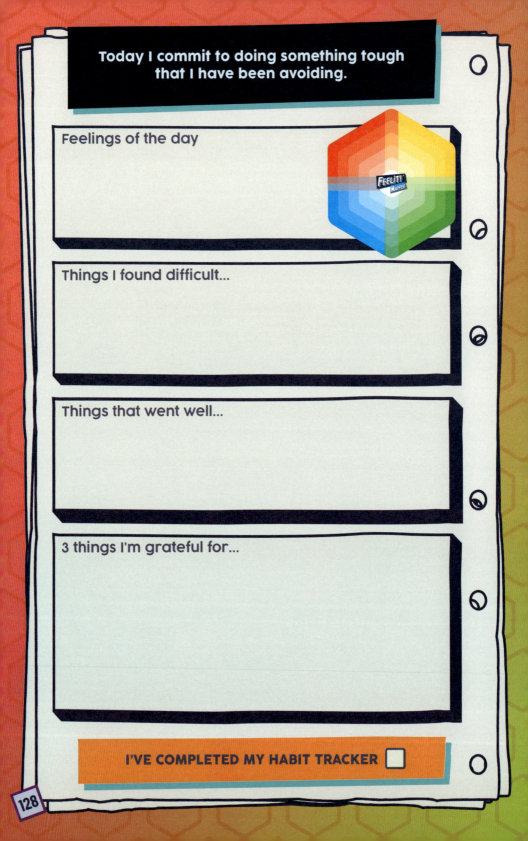

REFLECTIONS OF THE DAY

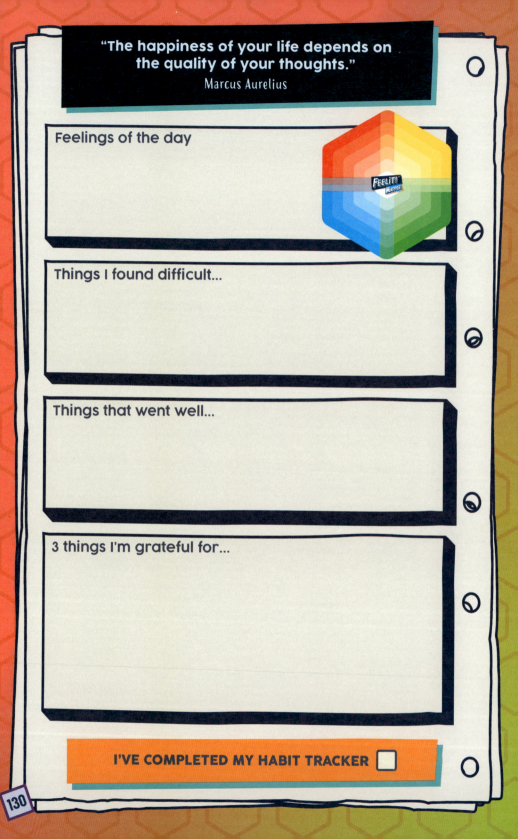

REFLECTIONS OF THE DAY

Today I will recognise my efforts and be proud of them.

Feelings of the day

Things I found difficult...

Things that went well...

3 things I'm grateful for...

I'VE COMPLETED MY HABIT TRACKER ☐

REFLECTIONS OF THE DAY

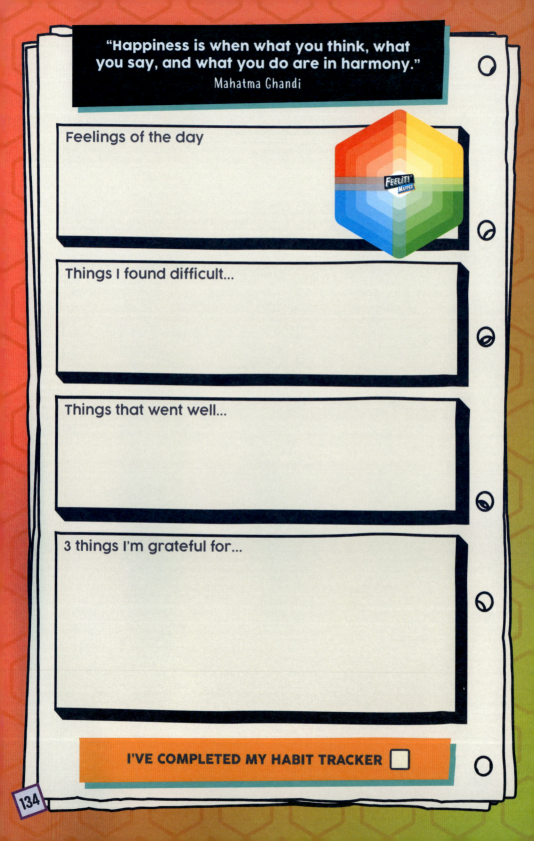

I choose to be friendly and patient with everyone I meet and treat them with respect.

Feelings of the day

Things I found difficult...

Things that went well...

3 things I'm grateful for...

I'VE COMPLETED MY HABIT TRACKER ☐

REFLECTIONS OF THE DAY

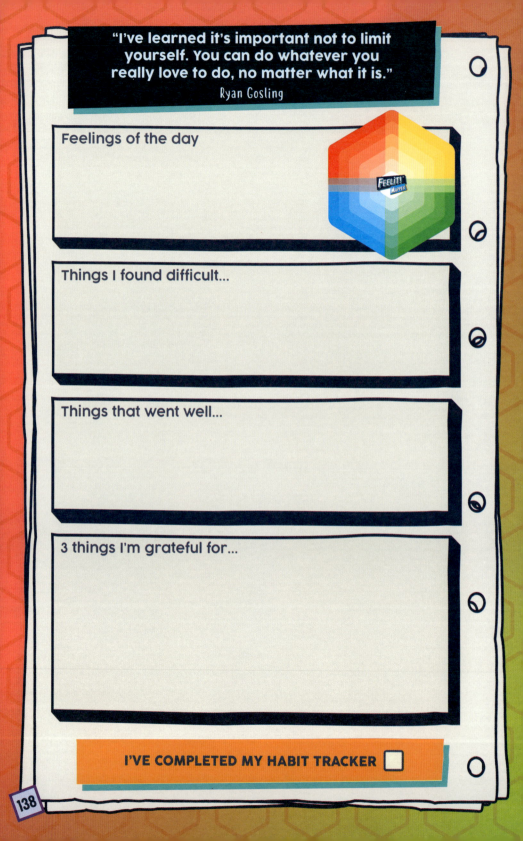

REFLECTIONS OF THE DAY

I choose to focus on the present and let go of the past and any worries about the future.

Feelings of the day

Things I found difficult...

Things that went well...

3 things I'm grateful for...

I'VE COMPLETED MY HABIT TRACKER ☐

REFLECTIONS OF THE DAY

REFLECTIONS OF THE DAY

I accept myself and my imperfections, knowing they make me who I am.

Feelings of the day

Things I found difficult...

Things that went well...

3 things I'm grateful for...

I'VE COMPLETED MY HABIT TRACKER ☐

REFLECTION TIME

It's time to stop, look back and reflect on what's going well, review any patterns (helpful and unhelpful) that are emerging and get yourself prepared for the next 10 days.

Look back over your journal for the past 10 days and make notes in the boxes below to help you track your journey.

Think about what affects each of these areas, are any patterns emerging?

Use the FEELIT Mapper to plot your feelings over the past 10 days.

➡️ Have your feelings mainly been:

☐ **Pleasant**   ☐ **Unpleasant**   ☐ **Bit of both**

➡️ What techniques have you used successfully to recover from unpleasant feelings?

WHAT WENT WELL?
Look at your successes and your Habit Tracker, what are the things that worked well and that you're proud of?

WHAT DIDN'T GO SO WELL?
What could you reduce to achieve your goals, such as procrastinating, unhelpful thoughts you may have, etc...

THINGS TO DO MORE OF

What are the things that bring you more joy or are most helpful to you in achieving your goals, or staying on track with your positive daily habits?

Consider the challenges you've had and how you can learn from these and move forward stronger.

GOAL SETTING

Based on your reflections, write down one or two goals that could help you become your best self.

Then, work out what positive habits you could focus on to help you achieve these goals.

MY GOAL	MY POSITIVE HABITS

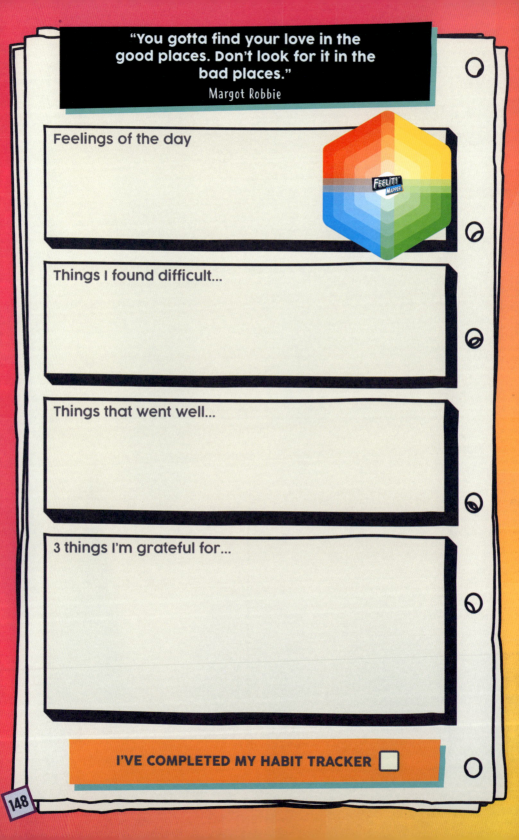

REFLECTIONS OF THE DAY

I have the power to shift negative thoughts into positive ones.

Feelings of the day

Things I found difficult...

Things that went well...

3 things I'm grateful for...

I'VE COMPLETED MY HABIT TRACKER ☐

REFLECTIONS OF THE DAY

> "Life is like riding a bicycle. To keep your balance, you must keep moving."
> Albert Einstein

Feelings of the day

Things I found difficult...

Things that went well...

3 things I'm grateful for...

I'VE COMPLETED MY HABIT TRACKER ☐

REFLECTIONS OF THE DAY

> "Believe you can and you're halfway there."
> Theodore Roosevelt

Feelings of the day

Things I found difficult...

Things that went well...

3 things I'm grateful for...

I'VE COMPLETED MY HABIT TRACKER ☐

I choose to push myself out of my comfort zone and achieve great things.

Feelings of the day

Things I found difficult...

Things that went well...

3 things I'm grateful for...

I'VE COMPLETED MY HABIT TRACKER ☐

REFLECTIONS OF THE DAY

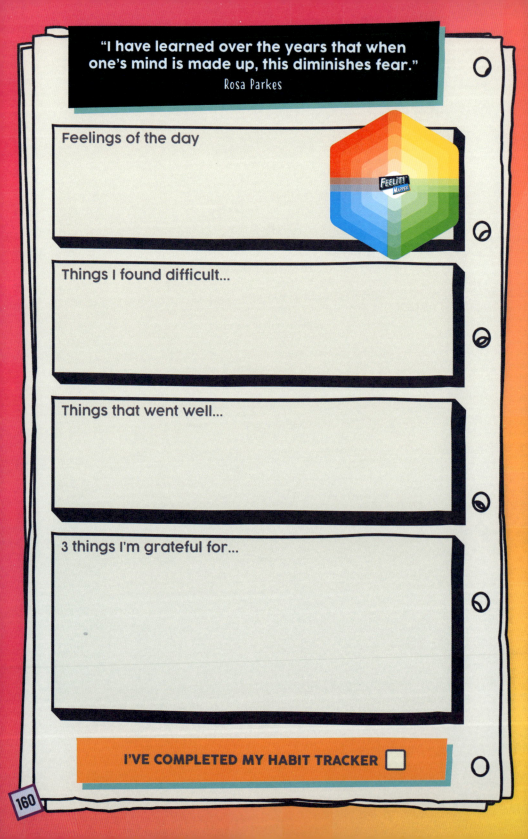

REFLECTIONS OF THE DAY

REFLECTIONS OF THE DAY

> "You will face many defeats in life, but never let yourself be defeated."
> Maya Angelou

Feelings of the day

Things I found difficult...

Things that went well...

3 things I'm grateful for...

I'VE COMPLETED MY HABIT TRACKER ☐

REFLECTIONS OF THE DAY

I practice gratitude for all that I have, and all that is yet to come.

Feelings of the day

Things I found difficult...

Things that went well...

3 things I'm grateful for...

I'VE COMPLETED MY HABIT TRACKER ☐

REFLECTION TIME

It's time to stop, look back and reflect on what's going well, review any patterns (helpful and unhelpful) that are emerging and get yourself prepared for the next 10 days.

Look back over your journal for the past 10 days and make notes in the boxes below to help you track your journey.

Think about what affects each of these areas, are any patterns emerging?

Use the FEELIT Mapper to plot your feelings over the past 10 days.

● Have your feelings mainly been:

☐ **Pleasant** ☐ **Unpleasant** ☐ **Bit of both**

● What techniques have you used successfully to recover from unpleasant feelings?

....
....
....

WHAT WENT WELL?
Look at your successes and your Habit Tracker, what are the things that worked well and that you're proud of?

WHAT DIDN'T GO SO WELL?
What could you reduce to achieve your goals, such as procrastinating, unhelpful thoughts you may have, etc...

THINGS TO DO MORE OF

What are the things that bring you more joy or are most helpful to you in achieving your goals, or staying on track with your positive daily habits?

Consider the challenges you've had and how you can learn from these and move forward stronger.

GOAL SETTING

Based on your reflections, write down one or two goals that could help you become your best self.

Then, work out what positive habits you could focus on to help you achieve these goals.

MY GOAL	MY POSITIVE HABITS

FINAL REFLECTION

FINAL REFLECTION

As this journaling experience comes to a close, it's time to reflect on your journey from the start through to the end.

Much like the 10-day reflection time, you're going to take a deep dive into what's happened, and see how you can move forward, with new goals and habits that will help you become the best version of yourself.

CELEBRATING MY SUCCESSES

WHAT WERE MY SUCCESSES?

WHAT DID I LEARN?

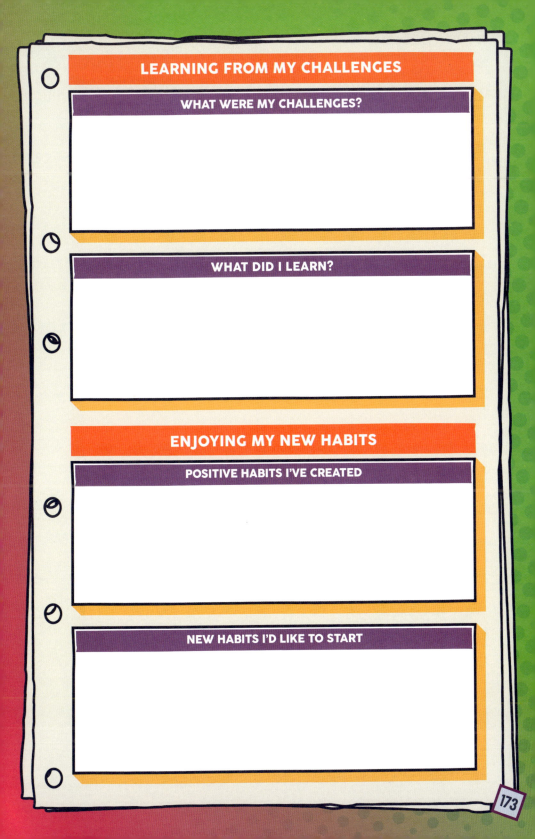

WHAT NEXT?

THINGS TO DO LESS OF

What are the challenges you've faced, the things that have been unhelpful to you in being optimistic, achieving your goals, and staying on track with your positive daily habits?

THINGS TO DO MORE OF

What are the things that bring you more joy or are most helpful to you in achieving your goals, or staying on track with your positive daily habits?

Consider the challenges you have had and how you can learn from these and move forward stronger.

THE POWER OF HABIT TRACKING

Time to consider who you are today and think about the habits you have that are not helpful to you, and what you'd like to do more of in life to help you THRIVE!

Habit tracking is an important tool to help people make small, achievable, positive daily changes that will increase their levels of happiness, confidence, and optimism.

To give yourself the best chance of success, you need to ensure you don't focus on the things you want to 'quit' or 'give up' but focus on the things you want to achieve or do more of. Taking this positive stance, will mean your energies are focused positively and your chance of success will be greater.

Think about the things that you can choose to do, things that you can easily achieve, things that will make your life better. Things that would be fabulous, small wins each day. Keep it simple, the idea is that you can succeed and get yourself into a pattern that can stick long term...

For example: 5 mins meditation, stay hydrated, be more assertive, digital downtime, focus in class, daily exercise...and so on.

ARE YOU READY?

The tracker on the right will help you map your habits every 10 days. You can carry through a habit if you want to continue tracking it for longer, or, add some new ones into the mix.

We've already added one key habit to each section... your ability to reframe your negative thoughts into more positive ones. The reason we have done this is because this key habit is vital in helping you be your best self every day.

We recommend you start small with just a couple of habits to track and add others over time. Remember not to be hard on yourself either, if you miss a day here and there, that's fine. The aim is to set yourself achievable tasks and timelines...we want you to succeed!